Table of Contents

Eggs and Nests.. 4

Life Cycle of a Chicken.................................... 22

Picture Glossary... 23

Index 24

To Learn More... 24

Eggs and Nests

nest

A hen is in her nest.

She laid eggs!

egg

Eggs have hard shells.

Some are white.

Some are brown.

Chicks grow
inside them.

Twenty days go by.
Chicks peck the shells.
They use their beaks.

beak

They hatch!
They are wet.

They dry.

Their feathers are fluffy.

They are soft.

Mom keeps them warm.

new
feathers

Seven days go by.
The chicks molt.
The new feathers
are smooth.

They follow Mom.

They peck at the grass.

They eat bugs.

rooster

At one year old, they are adults.

Adult males are roosters.

Adult females are hens.

This hen made
her nest in grass.

She keeps her
eggs warm.

Chicks will
hatch soon!

Life Cycle of a Chicken

A chicken's life cycle has three stages. Take a look!

egg

adult

chick

Picture Glossary

hatch
To break out of eggs.

molt
To shed feathers
and grow new ones.

nest
A place built by birds and other
small creatures to take care of
their young.

peck
To strike or pick up
something with the beak.

Index

adults 18, 19

beaks 8

chicks 6, 8, 15, 20

eat 16

eggs 5, 6, 20

feathers 11, 15

hatch 9, 20

hen 4, 19, 20

molt 15

nest 4, 20

peck 8, 16

roosters 18

To Learn More

FACT SURFER

Finding more information is as easy as 1, 2, 3.

❶ Go to www.factsurfer.com

❷ Enter "achicken'slifecycle" into the search box.

❸ Choose your book to see a list of websites.